Raíces, Relics, and Other Ghosts

Raíces, Relics, and Other Ghosts

Poems by

S. Salazar

© 2023 S. Salazar. All rights reserved.
This material may not be reproduced in any form, published,
reprinted, recorded, performed, broadcast,
rewritten or redistributed without
the explicit permission of S. Salazar.
All such actions are strictly prohibited by law.

Cover image by Elsa Muñoz (@elsa.munoz.art)
Cover design by Shay Culligan

ISBN: 978-1-63980-408-5

Kelsay Books
502 South 1040 East, A-119
American Fork, Utah 84003
Kelsaybooks.com

To mis tíos, especially Aunt Sarah, and Dad:

Thank you for sharing pieces of your lives with me,
even when it was difficult and painful. Your resilience
inspires me every day. I love you all tremendously.

To Abuela Ramona and Abuelo Natividad:

You did the best you could with what you had and what you knew.
Your stories and wisdom live on in those you left behind, in those
you never met, and in everyone who will come afterward.
Know that every breath and step I take to move forward
and every word I write is my way of saying *te quiero.*

Acknowledgments

I'm filled with gratitude when I think about the many people who have supported me throughout this project. First and foremost, the project wouldn't exist without the love and story sharing of my family, namely my Dad, Aunt Sarah, and Uncle Pete. Without your words, my words would be nothing.

I'd also like to thank my friend Solany Lara (@writewsoul) for brainstorming the title of this collection with me. Your feedback transformed this collection. Also, thank you Jillian Felgenhauer (@felgywritesfic) for spending months with me in coffee shops as I generated new work and organized the manuscript. This book wouldn't land the way it does without you.

Thank you to everyone in the writing community who hyped me up during the writing process. I'd especially like to express my gratitude to Alegria Publishing, a Latinx indie press based in L.A. With the guidance and encouragement of Alegria founder, Davina Ferreira (@davifalegria), as well as my amazing classmates, I was able to push myself as a writer. You all are the reason this book is out in the world. You all are also the reason I have found acceptance about my place within latinidad. I'm eternally grateful.

Thank you to my publisher, Kelsay Books, for your continual feedback and support. Thanks especially to Jenna and Delisa for answering my every email.

I'd also like to thank my editor, Jose Hernandez Diaz (@jose_hdz_dz), for your thorough work. Your lessons on form transformed these poems into more intentional pieces. You nourish the whole poet, and I'm a better writer for it. I look forward to our future collaborations.

Lastly, I'd like to extend my gratitude to the readers, editors, and judges of the journals that gave my poems their first home. I highly recommend submitting to and collaborating with the following journals, where earlier versions of these poems appeared:

The Acentos Review: "Tell Me," "Escrutinio," "Regreso," "Adaptada"

BOOTH Journal: "La lengua no tiene hueso, pero"

Latin@ Literatures: "Disconnect," "Imposter," "Why Choose Away?"

Midway Journal: "Endemic"

Poet Lore: "(English) Ivy"

Writerly Magazine: "Alegría"

Contents

I.

The Nature of Grief	15
Why Choose Away?	16
Just One Petal	17
Spring Wedding, 1942	18
Cada recuerdo	19
To Heal Roots	20
Rising	21
Disconnect	22
Garden Path Sentences	23
La lengua no tiene hueso, pero	24
Seguir adelante	25
Material Failure	26
Imposter	27
Range	28
I Am Not Damage	29
No soy daño	30

II.

Transplant	33
Home	38
Diaspora	39
Passed	41
Lost and Found	42
Hallow	44
Adaptada	45
Boxes	46
Down and Out	47
Tell Me	48
Rain	50
Unconventional Blade	51

Plumeria Rubra	52
(English) Ivy	53
Endemic	54
Artemisia Tridentata	55
Family Is	56
Combine All Ingredients	57
Bond	58

III.

Errar	61
Disintegrate	62
Shadowed Saplings Make for Weeping Willows	63
Semillas para entender	64
A Lifetime in Eleven Lines	65
Ghost Stories	66
Big Ask	68
Malagueta	69
Cycles	70
Regreso	71
Thistle I	72
Thistle II	74
Not in the Cards	75
What's Carried	76
De donde soy	77
Arraigada	79
Alegría	80
Moriviví aún vivo	82
Escrutinio	83
Petite	84
Legacy	85
Ghost	86
Resolutions of a Poet as a Mixed Latina	87

I.

The Nature of Grief

It often confuses people when I tell them I grieve
       the loss of a grandmother I've never met.

       I tell them our severed connections matter just as much
as polished ones. Even dead and decaying plants

enrich their ecosystem for the next generation of seeds.
       The system only works with living and dead together.

       Heritage is a spiritual ecosystem requiring both
present and departed to make a person whole.

Why Choose Away?

A woman in a rural house
curls into couch and crumbles in body.
She leans against Rocky Mountains, farm fields,
collapsed silver mines. Why would someone choose
to leave this wisp of woman in isolation away
from the distant echoes of her family?
There is a lone Latina in my house,
a cutting from plants rooted in islands and insomniac cities.
She aches for secondhand memories,
stained recipe cards, sepia photographs.
She will find a way to rewrite this story.

Just One Petal

I'm reaching for the light from the dark soil
that buries me. There's no telling whether my roots

will grow down or out or at all, whether my stem
will generate leaves or needles or anything.

I'm reaching for the light, except I can't emerge
from the darkness cradling me where there's safety in stagnant.

Something tells me I can grow in the dark like a peace lily,
just one petal to wrap around myself, to block the wind's currents,

to prove to the world that nothing's missing. But light
nourishes this body, igniting flames in my palms to cast light

on the roots of shadowed memories of shadowed people
capsuled inside me. The flames scorch the safety

curled around me, but what are a few burns but enlightenment?
What are a few blisters but knowledge? What are a few scars

but purpose? I'm reaching for the light inside, propelling me
toward a life where I'm no longer kept in the dark.

Spring Wedding, 1942

In this one, you are concrete. In this dull, pewter frame,
you smile at the camera. Your sepia eyes sparkle,
and your sepia curls coil down your back.
Grandpa's arms are around you, his lips bent in a smirk.

You may have been laughing. But I'll never know.
I'm left, as I always am, imagining the kind of grandma
you would have been. The kind of woman you were
and the kind of woman I could have grown up to be.

In this one, you stand a full foot shorter than Grandpa.
Your fingers wrap around a pale rose bouquet.
Your veil has white flowers on the top that puff out
like the clouds we daydream in. Each petal extends skyward,

for a bright future, for a place that's free.
Your dress sleeves expose only the tips of your fingers.
The fabric of your dress pools around your feet,
keeping you rooted to the ground. In this chapel,

you sow the seeds for your legacy. In this one,
you are not yet a mother, grandmother, or widow.
In this one, you aren't humming as you cook,
and your hands aren't shaking around a mug of Spanish espresso

alone in your kitchen. In this one, the wind doesn't carry you.
You don't bend against the elements. In this one,
you are a bariaco breaking through New York concrete,
your petals white and reaching for home.

Cada recuerdo

I hold inside about mis abuelos is rooted
       in memories that don't belong to me.

They are memories people don't want me to hear
       or have. Memories I have anyway. Whether in my mind

or in my DNA, my family's traumas shape generations—
       water spilled over a countertop. These memories fill pages

of mental scrapbooks on other people's shelves.
       Learning these stories is an act of rebellion. With work,

it will become an act of love, not a lesson of fates to fear.

To Heal Roots

Light spills onto pale cobblestone paths
and small store fronts painted sea foam green,

lilac, and salmon. Mangroves and las ceibas tangle
over top merchant carts. The eroded brick of El Morro

tells a story of times passed in waves.
Stepping past the cracked walls and faded murals

de la Iglesia de San Juan Bautista is a testament
to how time can't destroy what people have

the knowledge to fix. I scoop up loose sand
and soil into my palms in search of the roots

Abuela left for me to find one day. I sink my fingers
deep into the ground looking for the laceration,

looking to link to the long-lost land calling my name.
I'm trying to piece my future together from fragments

buried in the past, but I wish there was some sort of doctor
who understood roots and how to join them.

Rising

I come from sea salt and the Cascade Mountains.
I rise from rocky soil held together by roots
separated from the immense pines nearby.
I sprout into air thick with rain and mist
that clouds the views and paths clear to others.
I'm transplanted into summer dust and winter white,
to a "home" thousands of miles away
from home and places I can find it.

Disconnect

You aren't Latina, they say as the sapling is pulled up
from its place in the dying stump, snapped
near the base of the trunk. *You aren't Latina,* they say,

pushing the sapling's roots into new, distant ground.
You aren't Latina, they say to the sapling,
who could have grown just fine through the shrapnel of wood.

You aren't Latina, they say to the sapling, who could have
thrived, stretched into sky, rooted in the cleavings of scarred parts.

Garden Path Sentences

Betray us with words we're convinced we fully understand.
They deceive us with phrases and word orders rehearsed
      since grade school. Lead us down the beaten path of syntax.

We can't help but misinterpret: *La niña sent the story was pleased.*
Can't help but feign understanding: *We wrote the story with holes.*
      We jump to conclusions before a sentence's end:

Abuelo told us a little white lie will come back to haunt us.
We jump to conclusions to limit confusions:
      That Abuela was never here hurts.

These sentences require we reassess what we assume.
They demand we study all their parts, forward and backward
      and in extensive diagrams, to be understood deeply

the way they are.

La lengua no tiene hueso, pero

Its absence cuts a gaping hole even wider
when there's already not enough to fill it.
La lengua is like　　　　learning to walk—
we never step　　　　or stumble alone.
Our abilities grow　　　　in the presence
of others. La lengua　　　　en español is a tool
never taught to Dad,　　　　never taught to me.
No one nurtured us　　　　to know that Spanish
could take us places　　　　like English does.
We weren't shown how far　　　　the wings of español
　　could carry us.　　　　La lengua no tiene
hueso, pero sigue siendo
resistente.

Seguir adelante

If your language has limbs limp and brown,
don't clip the ends and hope they'll grow back

emerald and full of substance. If it refuses to climb
toward the light or leans over to one side, don't pin it up

and pray it holds. If its soil is craggy and dry, listen.
Don't water it the same way you've watered it

your whole life. Notice the water runs down the sides
of the pot and pools out the bottom. Change direction

and water its heart. Pay attention to its beats and lilts.
Don't demand it to thrive without changing anything.

Give it a reason to let water saturate the roots,
so those palabras puedan tener una salida.

Material Failure

There is something the matter when our matter,
which makes us matter, lacks the qualities
that make us individuals and collectively connect us
to one another. In the savanna, when mud dries and cracks
with a lack of water or root to string the pieces together,
it's material failure. Natural, but still failure.

Imposter

You hiding? Probably, but shouldn't be.
It's hard to step out into the sun's rays,

unsure you're deserving of its light. *You hiding?*
Maybe, but you don't belong in the shadows either.

You hiding? No. It's time to grow. You should
be here despite the fear, rising from the fields

to thank the world for your ghosts, rising up
from the mud to open yourself up

to voices bigger than yours.

Range

Our ancestors are forested mountains,
their roots wrapping around igneous rock.
Incessant winds bend and wisp through
the trees but seldom break them. We,
in the valleys, bathe in constant shadow.
Our limbs grow different at this elevation,
and the distance between us and those
mountain tops isn't something we ask for,
but a matter of plate tectonics. Trajectory.
Force. Destiny. Even within a close area,
those generations feel like foreign nations.
And we are their echoes.

I Am Not Damage

I carve myself away from damaged soil.
I refuse to be angry at my scars.

I confront them instead.
I won't allow hurt, confusion,

or resentment to consume me.
I'm not rain just because it's raining.

Even though I stem from past pain,
the stem is not pain.

I am a new beginning.

No soy daño

Me esculpo lejos del suelo dañado.
Me niego a enfadarme con mis cicatrices.

Me enfrento a ellas en su lugar.
No permitiré que el dolor, la confusión

o el resentimiento me consuman.
No soy lluvia solo porque está lloviendo.

Aunque procedo del dolor pasado,
el tallo no es el dolor.

Soy un nuevo comienzo.

II.

Transplant

I. To be moved with great force or upheaval.

    You grow where you're planted.
    Tall steel buildings, glass like a protective
    case, reflect a place so different
    from the island. Whitewall tires

    sputter through New York City streets—
    roots cutting through soil.
    Early on, there were beach days
    and large family dinners. But loss

    demands replacement.
    So Abuelo replaced failure as a father
    with liquor, and then failed further.
    Liquor took up the space where water and sun

    should have been, where love and son
    belonged. Over time,
    your dad yellowed, wilted, and died.
    You grew from one concrete crack to another.

    The skyscrapers surrounding you now
    shine brighter and tower the old.
    Those who enveloped you
    didn't resemble you or family lost.

    You no longer know the language
    and traditions because you were taken
    away from the household
    where they were practiced.

The soils of your childhood
didn't keep you connected
to Spanish or family dishes, didn't
give you the cultural ties

you needed to retain
what you left behind.

II. To settle elsewhere.

    You grow where you're watered.
    Bristle-barked palms bow from rough Atlantic winds,
    the ocean's roar fearsome enough to
    intimidate a woman to superstition.

    Salt-crusted seaside forts, cobblestone streets,
    and dirt paths through farmlands
    surround your childhood in Puerto Rico.
    I might never know why,

    but at 21, you boarded the San Jacinto
    for the Big Apple.
    You could have drenched yourself
    in a bustling city with everything to do.

    You could have watered
    the abrasive urban English,
    the Old Bay, and Broadway.
    Instead, you watered

    el español, arroz con pollo
    y bistec y cebollas.
    Sipped Café Bustelo with Abuelo
    at the formica table in your pale-yellow kitchen.

You didn't allow the proudest,
loudest parts of America
to swallow up the Boricua inside.
The walls of El Morro kept

Puerto Rico in but didn't keep
others out. You watered your daughters
with recipes and customs and family stories,
so the soil beneath their feet wasn't

the only thing defining them.
Your love ran deep, but you never returned
to the island. Did you miss where you came from,
or was it just easier to maintain tradition,

so the new wasn't as overwhelming?
Did you want to go back?
Did you not have the money to go back?
Did the people in your life hold you back?

Once, Títi told me
you could speak English,
but when your tongue stumbled
over our clumsy vowels

and silent e's, people laughed.
They didn't take you seriously.
They focused on the differences of your roots
instead of the mutual soil shared.

You weren't watered in English, Old Bay, or Broadway,
not in the land of the free and home of the brave.
You grew behind a barrier you built,
ivy racing over brick wall

and suffocating everything around it.

III. To replace something damaged or diseased.

    You lose the parts of yourself you don't water.
    Did you make mud pies in El Yunque?
    Did you play at the base of la Cordillera Central?
    Did you play catch in front of the Cappura Ruins?

    If you did, you sealed those memories tight
    between your teeth. You smothered out
    Puerto Rico's blue triangle with a flag
    whose stars excluded the island's.

    You suffocated your background and language
    in the name of America, free to repress yourself
    for English, whiteness, likeness.
    Abuela embodied every part

    of you that you chose not to water.
    She became an island in her own home
    because you feared the word spic,
    because you wanted tus hijos to grow up

    not feeling othered. You didn't
    want them to struggle like you.
    Abuelo, you chose to leave
    your soil in drought

    before drowning it in a bottle.
    You strove to replace your heritage
    and not contaminate your new life
    of patriotism, capitalism, colonialism.

When those ideals didn't take you in,
you replaced them with alcohol.
Your actions deteriorated you,
quickly destroyed you.

You robbed yourself of the chance to bloom,
and sometimes, I can't help
but wonder if this flowerless pattern
will continue

or end with me?

Home

Home was 170th street and 8th street,
Pike's Place and Glacier National Park.
Both pollution and wildfire smoke had squeezed air
from my lungs. Home was painting with Bob Ross
and building cardboard rocket ships to create a place
to breathe where *things happen for a reason,*
where *be safe* meant constant control of everything,
where Dad never hesitated in leading my eyes
toward the stars in search of the Big Dipper
but never to Abuela or Títi. No amount of cardboard
or Crayola crayons or packaging tape
built a rocket that could take me to them.
Now, home is a sequence of sound waves
from the East Coast to the West.
These waves carry Títi's crackling laughter
and is silent as memories of tostones fritos
smashed in paper bags and sofrito crushed in a pilón
lap the shores of absence knowing I'll never join Abuela
in her pale-yellow kitchen to share pollo guisado
and *te quiero* with her. Home is a lump in the throat,
knowing now that Abuela was a goddess.
She ran to catch the rain in outstretched arms,
thunder clapping at her back. Gratitude sprouts
from my chest knowing Abuela was the Atlantic,
never churning the same way or carrying the same current.
Hope blooms in my soul knowing I, too, can be an ocean.
I can be the Pacific. Or the Cascades.
Or El Yunque. Or flor de maga. Or myself.
Let me know when you get there.
Where you're home, you grow in the hearts of others,
where the unfamiliar steps through a door
to a place cast in shadow and lit by warm light.
Meet yourself there.

Diaspora

Take root, Abuela. I've seasoned the pans and polished
my español. Come find me and guide my roots
to proliferate into tradition and culture and language.
Help me germinate, even in the absence of nitrogen

and iron. Take root even though the conditions
aren't right. Take root, titís y tíos, where the soil's nutrients
aren't constant but are chaotic and displaced and thrive
an entire nation away. I'm growing in soil watered by tears

from Abuelo's fists, booze, and abandonment. Stories, take root.
Shower me in shouting matches and hiding beneath the table,
so I know which direction to grow. And not grow.
Take root, rusted rosary beads draped over Mother Mary,

where I wonder if I'd have something to hold on to if I grew into it.
Take root to Abuela's only photo where her black eyes
crinkle at the edges in a smile, where her hair spirals
unbound past her hips, where her husband still stands beside her.

Addiction, disease, obsessions, and compulsions, don't take root.
Take root, family traditions. Memorize Abuela's recipes
because there aren't any cards dotted with canola oil.
Recipes, take root so my kids can take root, and their kids

can take root. Gandules, guava, plátanos, sofrito, sazón,
take root and transform into stories that roll off the tongue.
Transform the narrative of this family. Transform me.
Take root, diaspora. Take root because I've been on this earth

too long to not know Boricua, but too short to let it
just die inside me. Isolation! Erasure! Assimilation!
Take root, decomposition, because it'll take a lot more
breaking down before I'm built up again, or maybe, for once.

Take root, time. Take root of this shrinking violet
and turn it into sage. Discarded pieces of what was,
take root to nourish what could be.
Nourish who could be. Take root.

Passed

Long after Abuelita left the island,
her parents passed on, and the family farm
was passed on to some faceless stranger.
Perhaps the farm was a wasteland after Hurricane Maria

stripped the roofs off houses faster
than tarps could be thrown on.
Or maybe it became something new:
a set of stark-white condos disguising the mounds

beneath which millionaires had hidden their fortunes.
Maybe the farm was only ever a story.
I'll never know because Abuelita passed on
the year before I was born. So suddenly

she passed on that no one thought to ask her
more about her past until it was too late.
I don't know much about her childhood,
and I don't know what happened to the farm

in Aguadilla where Abuelita y su familia
cultivated their lives. I don't even know
what they grew or raised or butchered there.
But one thing I know is I wouldn't have sold it.

Wouldn't put a price tag over preservation.
If I'd had the chance to step foot on family land,
I'd have planted my palms into the ground
and made something more of myself

and the seeds of stories I'm tasked to tend to,
what I'm tasked to pass on.

Lost and Found

If I found Abuelita's farm, I'd sift my fingers
through the sandy soil and long grasses to find an old,
paint-chipped board or crooked nail or rusted horseshoe
that marks where the old farmhouse once stood.

If I found that lone board or nail or shoe, I'd close
my eyes and travel back to hot summer days,
where kids' faces were stained with dirt
and the sweet stickiness of limber. In the afternoon,

they played tag in the yard, ran an obstacle course
in the vegetable garden. My smile would mimic theirs.
I'd open my eyes to the wild soils of now,
and I'd pull the weeds in our family's untended garden

to see where our roots meet. If I found the box
of family relics in my aunt's basement,
I'd bring its contents to light. Air it out,
clear it of cobwebs. If I found that box wilting

and water-logged and abandoned, I'd tear it open,
if it weren't torn already. Dive into it.
I'd run my fingertips across the wrinkled,
dust-coated photos of Abuelo and Abuela

sunbathing on the beach, laying on a sun-bleached blue towel
as their kids tossed sand in each other's faces
and down each other's swimsuits. The joy in these photos
would undo the knots in my stomach. I'd dig deeper,

analyzing the swooping cursive of birth certificates
and baptism records that signal the best of intent
before the mess. That signal beginnings when
I'd only heard the tragic ends. If I found an artifact

from either of their lives, I'd finally carry something real,
something loosening the tension in my body
while holding tight to this proof that mis abuelos
weren't some fable or old Greek tragedy.

Family relics remain hidden, and I remain a question mark
in the mirror, a reflection of when loss meets journey,
where someday I hope to see certainty.

Hallow

Mi abuela had every answer she ever needed
in the steeples, in the gold-leafed pages of the Gospel.

She molded her home in Genesis, John, and Job.
One day, a friend told me about helping her abuela

declutter an old bookshelf. A brown leather book tumbled
page-down, contents tossed to the floor. Faded sepia photographs

had been planted, abandoned family kept captive
in this hollowed-out Bible. Sacred pages swapped

for other sacred pages for decades. I celebrate her finding,
her knowing. Comment on how families will do anything

to bury their "burdens." Guilt gnaws my gut
as the end of learning about mis abuelos grows closer.

The inevitable dead-end preys on my mind, slays my ambition.
I can't help thinking about how much faster I'd pick up a Bible

if I could find the answers I seek within its pages.
Like my friend did. Like Abuela did. Like I don't.

Then, out of principle or desperation, I lower my lids
and send off a silent prayer to keep faith in this journey,

if nothing else.

Adaptada

Mi abuelita temía todo from black cats to ocean waves.
Mi papá temía las tragedias, and it shook him up just the same.

Mis miedos son agua covering three quarters of the planet.
But I've never feared the ocean, never let the whirring currents

keep me from dipping my toes in. Abuelita, si siguieras viva,
I'd tell you about the mangrove tree. How it roots itself

in an ecosystem that's supposed to drown it.
How its roots grow into the shoreline to protect fish

from predators hiding in the dark. How it keeps Puerto Rico's
resort-littered shores from falling into the sea in sheets.

How its roots can grow in agua, suelo y aire,
can grow thin and vertical and in loops.

Te diría estas cosas porque the mangrove's root systems
are adaptive, like how you strove to be before Abuelo's choices

stifled your transformation. Mi papá y yo, y tú hija también,
we've learned to adapt without you,

but we can't help imagining how we'd be if we rooted deeply
in the lapping waves to adapt with you.

Boxes

My bones are cardboard boxes, heavy when filled
and heavier when empty. The heaviest boxes

are tossed out the third story window
of Abuela's battered brick Hunt's Point apartment.

Her family had been rooted there for years,
but the green of her leaves wasn't the green

the landlord wanted. Abuela eyed
an entire lifetime, watched as cada foto

de su familia, mi familia, was swept against
black asphalt. Observed birth and baptism records

mingle with the elms along the Bronx River.
Witnessed family memory burrow deep

in flower beds. These empty boxes and lost contents
prick me with mysteries. They spur questions

that bleed on every page, where some answers
never can and never will have a solid resolution.

When boxes like these lie empty, we fill them
with fictions. We turn away and claim they're full.

Down and Out

People talk about being out of luck.
Floundering out in the weeds.
Breaking out in a sweat.
Breaking out in tears.
Being out for the count
or coming out ahead.
Feeling out of place.
Being out of time.
Going out on a limb.
But nobody talks about running
out of stories. That would be
out of the question.
We'd be told to pull out all the stops.
So, we'd be left to make a mountain
out of a molehill. Make a museum
out of a handful of memories.

Tell Me

Again. Weave the wisps of tales veiled in vines,
fading in age and disuse into something I can rewind
in my mind like a movie. Remind me that Abuela crushed
tostones fritos in a paper lunch sack with her fists.

That Abuelo constructed ships and shoved them into bottles.
Tell me how Abuela rubbed her feet together like sticks
that start a fire to keep her feet warm. How Abuelo was an artist,
a mechanic, before a drunkard. How they were both builders

and gardeners and pioneers. Fill me in about moving to the Bronx,
not staying in Puerto Rico or Venezuela or Spain
or wherever else in whatever new version of this story
you tell me this time. Recite to me the angle of Abuelo's fingers

as he flipped through a notepad to animate cartoons
at your hospital bedside. How Abuela's hums echoed the salsa
in her hips while she cooked dinner for a family still together.
Tell me again about the cocky teenage boy who marched out

to her farmhouse to serenade her. Tell me about her saying no.
Disclose to me the fragments of photos and documents of the lives
I never lived by. Create a verbal map. Count off the paces to where
I can find anything tangible to hold on to. Explain to me why

I hold on to what doesn't concern me. Show me how you
you made a mosaic from the broken pieces of your childhood.
Instruct me how to build something strong from the shards
of mine. *Please.* Tell. Me. Remind me how many tablespoons

of sofrito go in Abuela's pollo guisado, and where the crucifix
in her kitchen hung. Remind me it wasn't always this way.
That Abuelo pinched Abuela's butt and honked like a goose
because of some inside joke from an early date together.

That Abuela only ever wanted her husband and the life they started
building together. That their house didn't always shake
beneath frustration and fear. That love lived in the hearts
of the people who hurt you, who hurt me too.

Tell me again, because one day,
there will be no one around to tell me again.

Rain

I'm most connected to you in the rain.
When the sporadic droplets should place a curtain
of water between us, ellas deberían de ahogarlo todo.
But the water and the goosebumps on my skin

bring me to you. Behind closed lids,
the wheat fields of my hometown blur into Aguadilla,
into long expanses of plátanos, café y caña de azúcar.
Pequeñas casas de madera are loud with laughter

or a pan's sizzling oil, the tin roofs even louder
con la cadencia de la lluvia. When the wind tosses my hair
forward over my shoulders, I imagine you, mi abuela,
sixteen again, rushing past me, arms spread to capture the rain.

Mouth agape, you collect crystal droplets that tickle
your tongue to laughter. Todavía estás aquí.
You're still growing, the world around you is changing,
and you adapt with it. Todavía estás *aquí.*

When I open my eyes, your absence is drought.
A pesar de la lluvia, I question this sun-scorched soil.
I question the whipping winds and montañas escarpadas.
I question the worth of reaching up, rooting more deeply

into a place I'm not sure I belong, opening these petals
knowing no estarás allí to greet or guide me.
Thunder cracks behind me, and when I open my eyes,
I stretch upward. Yo agarro la lluvia y entiendo.

Unconventional Blade

Trauma
is a
spade
slicing
families
through
the roots.
People
don't
notice
damage
until the
plant
wilts
without
warning.
It tilts
over,
a ruin.

For plants, root damage is a death sentence. But
we're human. The waste underground is hidden.
What happens aboveground is a decision. We
choose to unearth what we didn't help create.
We stare at the toppled carnage we swore
to mend. We promise ourselves and our
children something better yet believe
the damage is too deep, overrun with
weeds. It's not the visibility of our
scars that keep us from healing.
Sometimes the rusted blades
we wield are the ones
we made our-
selves.

Plumeria Rubra

The plumeria is smooth, waxy white, a touch
of yellow at the center. I want to press it to my cheek
like the phone when Títi recites family recipes
and tales of Abuela's childhood en el barrio and Abuelo's desk

littered with illustrations. But when I place the plant
in my palm, welts form beneath the skin, burning below
the surface like fear. This journey through a broken past
to propel myself toward a whole future is a lonely one,

an odyssey where no one cares to understand
but everyone cares to question its worth.
Got me to question it too. If past people destroyed past versions
of present people, would the past uproot me too?

If mis abuelos hindered Dad's healing with heartache,
would I succumb to the toxic nature of their stories?
The weight of loss had pinned me to the ground.
The burden of my family's traumas convinced me

to carry the poisoned and the precious like they're the same thing.
But they aren't. They never were. Learn to let go.
Look from a distance. Look forward
without fear of looking back.

(English) Ivy

One summer, I swayed through
      twisting Oregon roads, through lush
      green forests. Even the ground was emerald.
          I said, *It's so beautiful here.*
          Does everywhere look like this?
      My friend answered, *It does, for now.*
      The ivy that grows here is invasive.
It won't look this way for long.

(English) ivy is a snake in the grass,
except it is both snake and grass
      to people who don't bother to ask.
          Its stem crawls across the ground
              and up the trunks of trees.
                  The edges of their leaves are teeth
                  biting scars into old growth forests.
            If they climb high, they cover the canopies
      and suffocate the lives they rely on to thrive.

      Whether by ship or covered wagon,
(English) ivy spread across oceans.
Made millions ancestors before their time.
      As I left Oregon, nearing the fields of home,
          I thought about the forests cut down to
              cultivate those crops. Then,
                  I thought back to (English) ivy.
              It looked magically emerald,
          but I knew the land was more
      vibrant without it, that we would
all be more vibrant without it.

Endemic

Ceiba, its roots slate gray, thin and tall like walls,
provided protection contra el sol sofocante.
Provided materials for the Taínos to build canoes with.

Its bark was solid but kept over rough waves.
Canoes inspired travel, fishing, tradition. No one bats an eye
if you can't catch a fish. Pero eres una anomalía

if you can't cook a family dish passed down generations
that somehow skips you. Even the best canoe can't navigate that.
Flor de maga, petals velvet, scarlet, size of a saucer.

La flor es el centro de una casa y una nación.
Destined to be decorative. Its roots know no bounds.
Crece en todas partes. This flora inspires substance.

Sustancia. Some people call it a hibiscus,
but the tree it flowers from is closer in kin to cotton.
La parte de ti that wants to bloom

would rather be la flor, pero tú estás la messy pale whirl of curls.
Estás desordenado. Fuera de lugar.
Tú tambien floreces. You soon will see it too.

Artemisia Tridentata

Sagebrush isn't named after Artemis because it's a hunter,
but because it's a survivor, because it plants the will to survive
harsh conditions into other living things. These oceans of gray
change with the weather and live to provide grouse and sparrows

refuge for a hundred years. They signal to each other
about incoming dangers, changing their leaves to be toxic
to their attackers. If only we could be so strong. But even Artemis
has lost her bow and arrows. When sagebrush is transplanted

away from their kin, they die within decades. Can't survive
without family nearby. Increasing wildfires destroy acres
of family plants. Makes it harder for populations to bounce back.
Sagebrush isn't some phoenix reborn from ash and neither are we.

We can't set ourselves on fire and expect to come back unscathed.
If we're going to grow through the damage, we'll need to nestle
into the places our ancestors took up space in. Without them,
we wither into something unrecognizable. We don't bounce back.

We won't be a guardian for anyone, including ourselves.

Family Is

-n't just trips to beach spits. Isn't being buried in warm sand
to be unearthed, unhurt and laughing. Isn't picnics in the park,

morning-chilled grass poking between fingers.
Isn't sunset hikes through pine forests behind the house.

Family is nightly dinners eaten alone. Christmases filled
with equal parts joy and grief. Hiding beneath the covers

from (another) fight upstairs. Family is dissonance—
in need of completion. Sometimes, every note and letter

endures time and distance and disguise. Other times,
those marks resonate too early or too late.

Other times, they don't exist at all. Luckily,
family isn't just a sound or collection of artifacts.

Family is a feeling that sprouts from belonging
and doesn't just stop when the sun won't shine.

Combine All Ingredients

My Norse grandmother has a book, paper crumbling at the edges
beneath its umber brown cover. This book contains my great

-great grandma's recipes. Blooms of chocolate cake batter
and water dot pages of faded pencil. Speckles of flour from a batch

of cookies over a hundred years ago are trapped in the binding.
I wonder if she used her best handwriting,

knowing her granddaughter would treasure this only keepsake,
or if the faded scribblings of recipes were so hard to read

because she thought no one would want them after she'd gone.
I don't know what she was thinking, but I'm here now,

and I look forward to the day I can replicate those molasses
cookies and almond cakes alongside Abuela's pollo guisado

y arroz con gandules. Recipes passed down to me without a book,
without flour stamps or fingerprints pressed into pages.

Cook the dishes that create just as much warmth as the recipes
written down. And one day, long after I'm gone, I imagine

a worn book of recipes left behind by me after decades of cooking,
flour and sazón and messy fingerprints dappled in the pages

of traditions someone else can cherish too.

Bond

I cultivate the connection between past and future.

I grip both and knot them together with poems

when the generation before prayed

that line be forever frayed.

III.

Errar

                    is
to step
through the
distant parts of
the world with wonder,
a choice to wander deliberately
to collect experiences, to move across
cobblestone paths and beneath flowering trees, to
talk to shopkeepers like you've been friends for decades, to
kick pebbles forward without stepping or
thinking back. But errar is about so much
more than this. It's to miss, to feel sick for
some home you've never stepped through,
never seen nestled in green fields, a place
you'd give anything to return to but can't
reside in because it had never been within
your grasp. To miss isn't just longing, it's
a miss, a blunder, a mistake. Errar is to err
on the side of wishful thinking. Errar seeks
a house not built in the way you imagined.
It wills a home that couldn't endure to exist
and give you everything you'd ever dreamed.

Disintegrate

Dad's memories about his parents can fit in the palm of his hand.
With each passing day, his calluses brush the rough edges
of memory, fraying them further. Despite the fray,
these memories are heavy. He had told me all he could,

but we both knew it wasn't much. When I asked mis tíos
about mis abuelos, hoping to give Dad more to hold on to,
hoping to carry some of the weight, they couldn't speak.
Or wouldn't. Their silence keeps the oldest, most pleasant,

most painful memories behind walls that span miles, years,
generations. Memories that once fit in Dad's hand are now mine.
Because they are my stories, not my experiences,
these palm-sized memorials will soon be reduced

to seeds pinched between finger and thumb.
When my children crave stories to cradle at night
they'll only get a pinch that will fray to a grain
that over time will become a wind whispering questions

and pulling future generations in directions they won't understand,
directions I'm just starting to grasp. It doesn't have to be this way.
Heritage shouldn't grasp for straws. Families shouldn't be secrets.
Holidays shouldn't have to happen at five different houses.

Conversation can be the system connecting us in times gone
and times still to come. Our histories and legacies
can be groves instead of the tools chopping them down.

Shadowed Saplings Make for Weeping Willows

My roots are shallow, barely skimming surface soil.
Beside me, the roots of towering willow trees
jut in and out of ground, a testament to time and tribulation.
Mis tíos are willows, their wings of leaves wide and deep.

The sun's rays no longer pierce through their canopies.
Somewhere up there the light of mis abuelos feeds
the willows. But from down here, I can't tell if this light
nourishes or scorches them, can't tell if their canopies are lush

or dry and crackling. On days when the wind is fierce
and forces the willow's stubborn branches to let in the light,
I feel the warmth of mis abuelos, the impact of their journey.
But I also feel the lonesome chill of their shadows,

shadows the willows want to forget, shadows some felt obligated
to protect me from and others thought to make monsters out of.
I've always been taught to not fear the dark, but never how to live
in it. Survive in it. Like they've had to. Like they didn't want

for their children, nieces, or nephews. Like what happened
anyway. I get that it's hard to discuss the shadowed parts
of the people who brought us light, or should have,
and it's even harder to let go. But anything's better than living

in a future left fallow, weeping in shade.

Semillas para entender

"When I meet somebody, I never meet that person as an individual. I meet their entire lineage."
—*Thich Nhat Hanh*

Fish who swim too close to the surface
                risk a fisherman's barbed hooks
                              or a hawk's daggerous claws.

People who wear honesty
                like a second skin know the sting
                              of others bearing truth as costume.

Some roots linger on surface soil.
                Won't grow deep or expose under
                              -bellies. Won't fight uprooting.

                But
            we are our
         roots, and they are
       us, and keeping bitter roots
     buried does nothing to plant
   seeds of understanding. Cling to
the sharp stones of our ancestors.
Sift fingers through the violence,
drugs, and alcohol toxifying soil.
Allow them all in. Thank them
    for their infinite lifetimes
      of lessons. Free them
        to free us too.

A Lifetime in Eleven Lines

Abuelo spent hours planting animations into notepads
to brighten his dark Bronx apartment, banked on the place

where dreams come true. They didn't. He built model ships
that resembled the ones he'd been on during WWII in the navy,

crammed them into bottles to keep his inner child alive.
But he couldn't. He emptied those bottles himself,

flooded his belly with alcohol until he left this world behind.
He broke his family with fists, and even the love of his wife

couldn't bring him home. Now we're all angry and long for home.
I know I cling to this story: a grandpa, a bottle, a broken home,

but it's the only one I have of him to tell.

Ghost Stories

I'd always feared the idea of ghosts,
the image of one floating down the hall
when I'd believed I was home alone
was enough to throw my quilt over my head

and pray their discontent led them away.
Led them home. Now, I chase them. Reinvent them.
I dip into the earth, cup clay in my palms,
and create the ghosts I've learned to fear.

I carve these apparitions into ancestors.
Late at night, when I drive over creeks and fields
named after the slaughter of Indigenous peoples,
I expect to see the Weeping Woman,

expect to see empty eyes, clothes wisping and white,
her frail fingers running through muddled waters
in search of answers or ever after. I predict
she'll be the woman I'd been warned about.

But the ghost I see is Abuelo. So, I predict
he'll be the man I'd been warned about:
a bottle in his hand, eyes red and fist clenched.
But I reinvent this ghost. Because his story

depends on the version people choose to tell.
The version people ask to hear.
Abuelo could've drowned his kids willingly
in rivers of liquor. Or we can tell his story

from a place of understanding, where his eyes
grew bloodshot from sifting through help wanted ads,
where guilt filled the family cupboards once full of food,
where he emptied bottles to create a river his family

could escape down. Then drowned. Wasn't around to save
himself or protect his kids from drowning themselves.
One Abuelo is vengeful, the other an oversight.
But chasing ghosts has shown me that either way

is a heartbreak to heal from. Together.

Big Ask

Never asked to be planted. Never asked to be planted *here*.
Didn't ask to navigate a world where unease was the norm.
Had no control of days' droughts followed by sudden hurricanes.
Didn't ask to watch others grow wise and confident while I stayed

stunted. Withered and warped in inconvenient conditions.
Never asked to care for others in ways I didn't care to be cared for.
Didn't ask to work so hard just to have so much hard work ahead.
But I did ask to be planted on this cracked pleather couch

in front of a pair of glasses and a clipboard who constantly asks,
And how does that make you feel? I answer honestly
because admitting those tough and painful and sometimes
impossible things is better than burying them
and hoping no one remembers to ask.

Is better than convincing the world my traumas never existed.
Is better than planting a seed in lifetimes of toxic cycles
and locking it tight, destined to be repeated.

Malagueta

Coping skills weren't passed down to me.
Never made it to our family tree. But Malagueta did,
in a way. This tree is protected by law.

New saplings planted daily to guarantee its safety.
Pero, ¿quién garantizó la seguridad de mis abuelos?
Who guarantees mine? Malagueta leaves are crushed

to make Alcolado. Bay rum. Relieves some aches and pains.
Cleanses energy. Protects the spirit. But alcohol
hasn't cleansed or protected my family in generations.

Abuela held a crucifix in her palms to cleanse her energy.
But even she couldn't pray the intrusive thoughts away at night.
Abuelo held a bottle to his lips to numb his aching spirit.

But even he couldn't escape the pain of his failures
weighing him down. Dad held what Abuelo did for decades.
Before, it was the bottle, but now it's just the pain.

But I can't let lifetimes of heartache guide me
toward some quick fix or turn me into the next addict.
Instead, I practice coping, hold tough discussions

con la niña pequeña I sheltered and shamed to feel unworthy.
I apologize, hear her out. And I hold tougher discussions
with the proud, self-reliant woman I will to appear in the mirror,

the one I'm learning to be cada día.

Cycles

The space in which my family occupies is a revolving door—
each rotation moves me further from their timelines.
Yet turning to push the door in reverse
won't take me back to a time with them:
to picnics beneath the Central Park oaks
or a game of tag among Puerto Rican palms.
I existed decades after Abuelo exited the door.
I stepped between the panes of glass
just as Abuela stepped out.
Abuelo took everything with him except his family.
Abuela held tight to her Latin roots,
clutching memories of a childhood in Puerto Rico.
Lugged them through her new life in America
until they calloused and cracked her hands.
Stubborn, she carried that heritage out the door.
Took customs and superstitions and stories.
I'm left alone, spinning with the echo of her lifetime
in empty air, the dust of her travels clustered on the floor.
Pressing my palms against glass where her prints had been.
Willing my prints to match hers. Praying I leave something more
behind despite having less. One day, I'll step out.
Everybody does. But I can't leave until I fill this place
with something more than dust.

Regreso

I'd rather give someone the scenery than ask them to imagine it up
when they don't understand this world, this disconnect from it.
In ink, muses sprout into memories that sprout into messages.
As my ballpoint pen bends and curls to form stories in stanzas,

mis abuelos existen de nuevo. Estas palabras son su regreso.
La oportunidad de una vida que nunca imaginarón que podría
ser suya. When I write, I see a woman who loves hip-length hair,
a bold red lip. When I create, I see a man who likes pressed slacks

and Old Spice. But I also see a broken marriage. Heartbreak acting
as a model for their children. Este dolor proviene de las lágrimas
de la abuela cuando pierde todos sus sueños. Lágrimas que caen
sobre sus hijos. Lágrimas que invaden los corazones de sus hijos.

Los corazones de sus hijos se transforman en dolor.
Esas heridas se convierten en personas que hieren a otras personas.
El pasado no es el final cuando nosotros somos los nuevos
comienzos. Mis tíos don't pull pen across paper like I do.

They conceal the memories, so they don't come to life again,
but those memories never died. They live because we've survived
every bitter word and impulsive action mis tíos couldn't bury,
the reverberation of dysfunction exposed in their tone.

They chose to stay the course and repeat those patterns,
but I'm choosing to rewrite this story.
I'm opting for a change in scenery.
Estoy tomando lo que no se puede matar

y lo estoy nutriendo en algo más saludable.
Más consciente. Más resiliente. Más fuerte.

Thistle I

Speaking Spanish should create an outpouring of warmth
to fill the empty spaces where Abuela should have been.
Where her lessons should have been. Where I could have
sat in her lap as she read to me in a language binding

our existences together. That world never existed.
Never would. Now, I'm an island of diaspora in the sea
of America where speaking Spanish is shame. Not for me.
Yet when Spanish leaves my lips, it scuffs and cuts

stumbling clumsily out of my mouth. This shame is a thistle,
the jagged edges of this weed leaving lacerations when uprooted.
Last fall, in Mexico, I was asked if I spoke Spanish four times.
By four different people. Each time, I said no. *Your accent is good,*

my cab driver called through the rearview mirror.
And still, I said no. The few phrases and verb conjugations
I could recall weren't nearly enough to reply, *Yeah,
I speak Spanish,* without feeling like a liar. Actually being one.

Each no was a new thorn digging into my ribs,
the little spines piercing the parts of me too spineless
to keep my gaze up through the mistakes and mispronunciations
that show I'm growing. Amidst the background of car tires

bumping over cobblestones and hundreds of columns of tequila
rattling in their shelves, a clerk asked if I spoke Spanish,
his eyes shimmering with amusement or curiosity or hope.
I admitted my shame for the third time that day,

but instead of accepting my answer, he tested my Spanish.
His rapid words wormed into my ears, and my thoughts swam
as if my head was forced underwater, but I made out
the word entiendo. Irony is only understanding the word

understand in a sentence rooted in words and worlds
I've never understood and might never truly understand.
It's a shame with roots so deep that trying to upheave
the pieces means some are inevitably missed.

Thistle grows where remnant roots lie, and shame
isn't eradicated at once or over time or ever.
Pero siempre vale la pena intentar entenderlo.

Thistle II

Back at home, surrounded by farm fields, strip-logged forests,
lifted pickups, and seas of plaid shirts and camo pants,
I reflect on living in rural America, where nobody
asks me if I speak Spanish because nobody
here speaks Spanish, because Spanish
speakers don't live here, and that
is a whole other thistle to uproot.

Not in the Cards

These cool glossy flash cards are a compass,
each guess a change in trayectoria—one pile a victory,
and the other a tall reminder of your inability
to remember the most basic words and phrases.

Your knees bow beneath you, shoulders slumped with fatigue.
The blades of carpet cushion your cramping legs as you sink
further into memorizing: hola, niña, jugar, lápiz.
No amount of hard work can cushion the blow

of peeling back plastic wrap on a vocabulary card deck
meant for three-year-olds, of still not using estar or ser
correctly when you need to, and you always need to.
You waver over every spoken word. You listen to your amigos

speak Spanish only to hear radio static. You switch
to English the moment you feel buried, or you never shift
to español in the first place. Fire flares across your face,
not embarrassment but shame. Fallar por un tiempo.

Cuando algo isn't in the cards, that doesn't mean it won't be later.
Your path is a series of choices. Tu vida isn't what's likely
to happen. It's what you make happen. Así que haz que la vida
suceda. Cultivate opportunity. Develop destiny. Agárrate fuerte

a esas tarjetas y conéctate con la versión de ti que sabe estas
palabras de memoria, igual como lo hicieron tus abuelos. Léelas
como si tu vida dependiera de ello. Porque así lo es.

What's Carried

How I carry my roots is how I'll carry everyone
in my heart forever onward. How I handle the past
is how I'll heal. And if I don't handle it, if I don't heal,
then the past will handle me. Pupils clouded in melancholy,
unable to turn my head toward the fruitful orchards ahead.
It's not my responsibility. It's my *honor* to shoulder this healing
and guide an entire lineage to infinite peace.

De donde soy

Soy de sazón y gandules,
y de cada comida con carne.
Soy de un idioma que bloquea mi mente de mi lengua.
Soy de icy ocean swims and solitaire,

de Little Golden Books and Disney Channel Movies.
Soy de *Don't give up, we worked hard*
so you didn't have to y *Did you try hard enough?*
Soy de wide toothed combs,

graphic T's, and secondhand jeans.
Soy de tire swings and parrot wings.
Soy de kite festivals and family dinners
at a long oak table under one roof.

Soy de Abuelo, who drowned
hope in what he drank
when the world felt too troubled.
Soy de Abuela, who never stopped waiting

for her loved ones to return home.
Soy de a family tree lacking roots.
Soy de roots I'm not convinced exist.
Soy de a half-brother I never knew

before addiction found him too.
Soy un graduado universitario
de primera generación.
Soy de una generación who knows

toxicity outside of
blood-alcohol level.
Soy de coastlands and grasslands,
de latinidad y americana.

Soy a single sepia photograph
mixed with the bottoms
of a hundred bottles
mixed with the desire

to do better.
Soy moments I never had
with people I never got to meet.
Soy la hija de la diáspora.

Arraigada

My roots are things of legend, not because my ancestors
descend from Odysseus, but because my roots are fabricated

from stories. Some thrift store quilt, squares not even mine,
something anyone could find and piece together in time.

Roots not fragmented. Lost. Absent. Without roots,
a tree can't survive. Sections of canopy will dwindle down brown.

A light breeze will topple it, exposing a trunk unanchored.
I may have been rootless, but I'm learning to build them.

I ship in ingredients to prepare my own identity,
tear recipe cards into roots and papier-mâché them with sofrito.

Construct roots that burrow deep. Bury them. Water them
with Abuela's mother tongue porque mi comunidad coaches me

to use it. They encourage me to weave whole stories from the true,
holed ones. Instead of steering me away from latinidad,

like the orphan Boricua that I am,
they extend their hands and lead me to her spirit.

Alegría

Over years and decades, we climbed mountains
for alegría only to find ice and stone. We parted seas
of corn-filled fields for alegría only to find soil disturbed
by gentle spring winds. We swam to the bottom

of frigid turquoise lakes for alegría. We scooped up
the silt only to find arsenic mixed with sand.
We'd been convinced alegría was myth,
but it isn't. Because when we start to sift

through all the toxins, we forget to lift our spirits
to nurture alegría. We neglect to try something new
or risky when it's so much easier to stay the course
despite the promise of alegría if we branch out.

So alegría isn't myth. It's a choice. A life-long quest
in changing mindset. A practice in not letting the heavy
weigh us down, not letting the promise of a brighter day
dictate how we spend our darker ones.

Alegría demands we create our own light.
We didn't know how many left turns or secret streets
it would take to get to alegría. And when we found it,
we weren't sure if we could reside in its light.

Now, we know we've always belonged with alegría
because we unearthed the joy we'd buried.
Exposed the battle between previous pain
and future prosperity that kept us from being free.

Exhumed the past and the ancestors that lived there
without letting them pin us to their traumas.
Now, with alegría, we give the gift of presence
to our future selves. With alegría, we're gifted

a place where the dark can't overshadow
the light we bring.

Moriviví aún vivo

My family's past isn't mine to carry,
but it also isn't mine to forget.

Turning my back on the facts won't lessen the load.
The weight of my grandparents' words aren't mine

to hold in my heart. I won't stand still as the curse
of being our own destruction rushes at me.

I'll be a moriviví, blooming up and out and with spines.
But I'll also be the moriviví that refuses to close

in darkness or under pressure. I won't curl
in on myself, waiting for a dazzling new day.

I'll be open and vulnerable to what's lurked
in the dark for generations.

And I won't let it determine my form.

Escrutinio

De niña, I hated my eyes. Siempre criticándolos.
Asymmetrical and tired, too wide-eyed or not open enough.
Hooded lids eyeliner couldn't redesign into something striking.

Para reírse, I referred to myself as so full of shit my eyes
turned brown. Deep down, I believed that joke held the truth,
especially when surrounded by eyes ocean blue in a sea of white.

I never understood mis ojos, how they're Spanish espresso,
fuerte y distinguida like Café Bustelo, how they're desbordante
like El Yunque's forest floor after rain. The circles under my eyes

are bruises from fighting back the silencing
of Borinqueños for centuries. These purple half-moons
are family heirlooms of sleep tossed and turned like the sea,

rooted in nervios y desplazamiento. Decades of eyes
that I couldn't see before. Dad's eyes. Abuela's eyes.
Brown eyes that glimmer, showing fight and might,

ojos que albergan eternidades en un abrir y cerrar de ojos.

Petite

When I feel small,
incompetent, and meager—

when I feel miniscule,
unwanted, a weed
trampled beneath feet—

when I feel undeserving
of the space I occupy,

I stop.

Pin shoulders back.

Not every nieta
experiences
the world through
their abuela's eyes.

Pero I do.

Y de esa manera,
soy hercúlea
Ilimitada.
Infinita.

Legacy

At the end of my days, I'll peer in the mirror
and joy will cushion the blow ends bring.
My many smile lines will grow into ranges
of smile mountains. I'll be proud to see Abuela
alongside my mom in the landscape of my features.
Proud to keep them with me. Pride like I long for
my daughters to feel when their bones grow tired,
when they see the memory of me staring back in the mirror.

Ghost

Orchids refuse to be confined to a single shape, color, or location.
Their petals sometimes mimic monkeys or insects or ships.

But the holy ghost orchid is only ghostly in spirit.
Grown in soils oversaturated with water, this orchid shoots

from the ground with petals shaped like a white bird soaring away
from suffocating bog water and layers of leafy decay.

Also called the white egret orchid, this flower has wings.
Yet it chooses to remain attached to its stem lodged in things

left long ago. It stays suspended between root and sky,
between gone and going. Despite knowing this, it doesn't wilt,

doesn't strive to sever from the festering. The little spirit bird rises
higher, rocking softly in clouded sky. Unlike this bird, I used to try

to leave decay behind. Now, wings spread in the in-between,
I open my mind to the balance of simply being.

Resolutions of a Poet as a Mixed Latina

At the end of este libro, I'd wanted to stand on a mountain
and pin its pages to the summit and scream, *I've finally arrived!*

But I haven't, and I never will because I'll always be learning,
practicando, growing into places where I want to take up space.

I'll devote décadas pruning myself back when I've overstepped
or misunderstood yet another facet of mi vida en latinidad.

I'll stumble and stutter para siempre, but I won't waste
another second closing myself up or closing out unstable español

or ignoring painful thoughts when they wonder
about being Boricua and what happened to mi familia

that crushed our connection to la isla and each other.
Mi vida in diaspora will be never-ending, a link of DNA—

lifetimes of ache and mistakes without concrete answers
or reasons why—all held together by last name,

hearing, and healing, so it no longer hurts to hold,
so la próxima generación will want to hang on to whatever's left.

About the Author

Raised in the Pacific Northwest, S. Salazar has always felt at home in the mountains. As an educator, she strives to show people that success isn't defined by background.

S. is published in *Harpur Palate, The Acentos Review, Booth Journal, Poet Lore,* and elsewhere. Her work explores generational trauma, identity, Latinx heritage, diaspora, and mental health. *Raíces, Relics, and Other Ghosts* is her debut poetry collection.

When she isn't writing, she can be found hiking with loved ones, talking to her parrot, Gizmo, and gushing over every dog she sees.

Follow her @writessalazar on Instagram and Twitter or online at: writessalazar.com

About the Artist

Elsa Muñoz is a Mexican American artist born and raised on the South Side of Chicago. She credits her interests in nature and healing to her experience growing up in an underserved and often unsafe community with little access to green spaces. Spending most of her childhood indoors led to the cultivation of a rich inner world in which she could find beauty and sanctuary. Her work explores the threads connecting ecology, culture, and spirituality.

Muñoz received her BFA in oil painting from the American Academy of Art in 2006. She's since had 11 solo shows, including at the National Museum of Mexican Art (2011) and at the Union League Club of Chicago (2016), along with group shows throughout the U.S. She was recently awarded a SPARK Grant from the Chicago Artists Coalition (2022) and was the recipient of the Helen and Tim Meier Foundation for The Arts Achievement Award (2019). Notable collections include the National Museum of Mexican Art (Chicago), North Park University (Chicago), and the private collection of Martin Castro, Chairman of the U.S. Commission on Civil Rights under President Barack Obama.

Follow her @elsa.munoz.art on Instagram or online at: elsamunoz.com

www.ingramcontent.com/pod-product-compliance
Lightning Source LLC
Chambersburg PA
CBHW031202160426
43193CB00008B/473